Cognitive Behavioral Therapy for Beginners

How to Use CBT to Overcome Anxieties, Phobias, Addictions, Depression, Negative Thoughts, and Other Problematic Disorders

By Madison Taylor

Table of Contents

Chapter I: What is CBT?

Life can be sad, and therefore some thoughts naturally make us sad. Thinking about a death in the family or the loss of a house in a fire naturally are depressing. It is OK to feel sad about truly horrible events. When someone wrongs you, it is normal to be angry and resentful. Everyone also has moments of fear when their lives appear to be in danger.

But constant sadness, anger, or debilitating fear can indicate that there is a problem in your thinking. For instance, if you get sad when a friend cancels plans and start thinking that no one likes you, there may be a problem. You are taking normal situations and blowing them up to be extreme in your mind.

You are basically creating thoughts that lower your mood and have a negative effect on your overall life. Normal situations should not distress you, and if they do, you may be in need of cognitive behavioral therapy.

If you suffer from depression, anxiety, or anger problems, you most likely have too many negative thoughts in your head. You have unhealthy thoughts patterns that put you in a constant state of emotional agitation. If you struggle with addiction or phobias, often these are symptoms of deeper underlying disorders in your thinking. That is where cognitive behavioral therapy can make all the difference in your life.

Cognitive behavioral therapy, or CBT for short, is a form of therapy that attempts to identify negative thought patterns in your mind and correct them. This therapy is employed by some of the most highly educated shrinks, but you can also employ it yourself to make a wonderful difference in your life. CBT allows you to gain control of your mind and stop the thoughts that make you depressed, anxious, or angry all the time.

Few people are actively aware of their thinking patterns, even though they engage in these patterns every day. This lack of self-awareness can lead to many problems. Thoughts govern your emotions and your actions, so constant negative thoughts caused by unhealthy thought patterns can wreak havoc on your life. By using cognitive behavioral therapy, you gain awareness of your thinking and actively work to correct it.

When in therapy, a therapist will have you talk about your problems. As you talk, you subconsciously reveal thoughts that lay behind your problems. For instance, if you feel lonely, you may reveal in therapy a lingering belief that you are unlovable. Your therapist is trained to point out the fallacies in your logic. When you utter your innermost thoughts, he or she may point out something like, "But what makes you think that you are unlovable? Do you really believe that you are so horrible that no one can ever love you?"

The beauty of CBT is that you do not have to pay a therapist hundreds of dollars an hour to find out what your real thoughts are and how these thoughts are incorrect. You can unearth these thoughts yourself and address the fallacies in your own logic. Using a journal or self-talk, you can go over situations, discover the thoughts that lie behind your feelings, and realize what group of negative thought patterns your thoughts belong to. Once you realize that the way you are thinking is simply untrue, you can work to replace your thoughts with more healthy ones.

CBT breaks negative thought patterns into clusters known as cognitive distortions, which we will discuss in more detail in Chapter V. There is always a better alternative thought to each negative one. This book aims to help you identify your bad thoughts, replace them with healthy thoughts, and thus be able to move forward with your life more happily.

By converting your negative thought patterns to more healthy ones, you will gradually get into the habit of healthy thinking overall. You will become a more positive person and your contentment in life will increase. This can eliminate mental issues, such as depression and anger. This can also help you take control of your life and live the way that you really want.

You will be amazed at how negative your thinking really is. Your thoughts have tremendous control over you, and negative thoughts naturally make you a negative person. When you start to employ CBT, you will begin to see how much you really do play a role in setting your own moods. You will also see where your symptoms and your behaviors truly come from. As you begin to change your way of thinking, you will notice that you change as a person overall.

If the true negativity of your thinking amazed you, you will be even more amazed by how much positive thinking can enrich your life and bring sunshine into your spirit. With control of your thoughts, you will find that you can attain pretty much anything that you want. Suddenly, the situations that used to destroy you emotionally will be much easier for you to cope with. Your symptoms, such as panic attacks and fits of uncontrollable rage, will suddenly vanish as you learn healthier coping mechanisms. Your mind will no longer run wild with thoughts and your behavior will no longer seem to emerge from nowhere; rather, you will have great control over all aspects of yourself and your life. This control is a great feeling.

Cognitive behavioral therapy allows you to address errors in your thinking to correct your behavior and in turn change your life. With this greater awareness of your own thoughts, you can really get to know yourself and how you want your life to be. CBT lets you become aware of the situations that you need to avoid to stay happy. It helps you develop coping mechanisms that enable you to tackle all of life's problems. You can really grow as a person using CBT on yourself.

But how can you use CBT on yourself if you are not a trained therapist? Is there a risk of making a mistake and screwing yourself up? Read on to learn how to safely and effectively apply CBT to yourself.

Chapter II: How does it work?

Cognitive behavioral therapy works by transforming your thinking patterns in the hopes of improving your mood and your overall life. While CBT is based on theory, its real-life applications have indicated a high rate of success. This is why CBT is a very popular therapeutic approach taken by many counselors and psychologists with patients.

The theory behind CBT is that your thoughts greatly influence your emotions. What you think has a dramatic impact on your feelings. Even a single thought can create a violent burst of emotion within you. Now since humans are believed to think at least seventy thousand thoughts a day, that means that you feel at least seventy thousand bursts of emotion throughout the course of your day. Negative thoughts are believed to lead to negative emotions, such as sadness and anger. If you frequently think negative thoughts, you are feeling nearly constant bursts of negative emotion throughout the day. If you feel more negative emotion than positive emotion, then your mood is obviously going to be lower overall.

CBT believes that repeatedly subjecting yourself to bad feelings from negative thoughts lead to your emotional suffering. When you exist in a state of constant emotional suffering, your life can become rife with problems. You can also develop mental illnesses such as depression, anger, and anxiety because your constant low mood influences the chemicals in your brain.

Life is much harder for people with mental illness because mental illness leads to poor judgment and physical symptoms such as lack of energy. You may not be able to live a fulfilling life if your low mood and negative thoughts are constantly zapping your will to live and your ability to function.

You don't have to suffer from your thoughts, however. It may not feel like it, but your thinking is totally at your disposal. You have control over your thoughts. If they seem to run wild, this is simply because you have not developed the strength you need to control your thoughts.

This is how CBT can really help you. This therapy approach trains you how to take control of your thoughts. With this control, you can

make your thoughts more positive and reject the
negative thoughts that bring you down. You can
begin to heal your emotional wounds and
recover from your mental problems if you are
more positive. Imagine how good you might feel
if you experience seventy thousand bursts of
positive emotion rather than negative emotion
throughout the day. Imagine how great life will
be.

CBT is goal-oriented. It guides you to
make firm resolutions to change your life. You
are encouraged to find problems in your life and
then find solutions rather than sitting around
feeling miserable. CBT thus gives you the power
to change your mind and solve your problems
just by adjusting your thinking. Instead of
thinking about how awful you feel about a break-

up or problems at work, you can learn to think instead of how to make your relationship or work better. Overcoming and removing problems from your life will also make your thinking more positive because you have fewer stressful burdens weighing on your mind.

Randomized empirical studies have proved that CBT works. Various studies have been conducted on patients receiving CBT and patients not receiving CBT to see the difference that the patients experienced with their mental health. The results were then combined and analyzed to yield the conclusion that in simple English says: CBT really works. Patients who received CBT had faster results in recovering from their mental illnesses than patients who did not. CBT is actually able to change people's thinking and treat their mental disorders.

Five years ago, a psychoanalyst named Dr. David M Allen attacked CBT as a "simplistic approach that only treats simple problems." Sadly, Dr. Allen underestimated CBT. Studies have proved that CBT works, even if it is simplistic. Perhaps a simplistic approach is the best approach to the complex issue of mental illness. CBT also deals with very serious issues. The emotional havoc that thoughts wreak on you have serious consequences, such as mental illness, and CBT addresses these problems. Dismissing CBT as a silly new fad is missing out on a great method of healing.

After reading all of this theory behind CBT, you may be skeptical. CBT sounds so amazing that it must be very hard work. How can you possibly do all that by yourself? Read the next chapter and you will find out that performing CBT is surprisingly simple. So simple, in fact, that you can do it on yourself.

Chapter III: How Can You Perform CBT on Yourself?

You don't need a pricy therapist to reap the benefits of CBT. The hands-on aspect of CBT makes it great and easy for use on yourself. Using CBT on yourself is how you can take control of your thoughts and thus of your life. You can perform actual work that results in better feelings and a better life. Seeing the rewards of your efforts is a great feeling and will make you love CBT.

To begin CBT, you must first resolve to commit to this therapy approach. CBT takes dedication and effort. Consider CBT the same as forming a new habit. It is like a workout routine, where you are conditioning and strengthening your mental muscles. You are training your brain and you need to commit to working out.

Next, you need to start working on identifying your thoughts and the situations in your life. You need to have full disclosure with yourself. This is an exercise in self-honesty and self-exploration. Even though there may be thoughts you don't want to admit to having, you must be honest about these thoughts to yourself in order to address them. You need to realize all the negative thoughts you have in your head.

You can do this in your head, but worksheets and a journal are far more helpful. Many anger management classes employ simple worksheets that ask you to write down situations that make you angry, what you think and feel, and how you could have handled the situation differently. Basically, you will want to fill out this exact same information in your journal or on a CBT worksheet.

You can download CBT worksheets online; a great source is found at this link: http://www.getselfhelp.co.uk/step1.htm. Another helpful method for CBT is to use an app called "Cognitive Diary CBT Self-Help" made by Excel at Life. This app is available for Android and Apple and provides a template for you to fill out that hits all the points you need to hit when analyzing your thoughts. For on-the-go people, having a journal in app form takes the inconvenience out of doing CBT.

You don't have to use a worksheet or app, however. A simple notebook and pen will suffice. Be sure to hit the following points:

What happened?

What did the situation make you feel?

What level is your distress? (Rate it from 1 for calm to 10 for panic and despair)

What cognitive distortions are you applying to this situation?

How can you think about it differently?

How can you handle this situation in a way that is helpful?

Now how do you feel?

What level is your distress now? (Rate it using the same scale as above)

When filling out your journal, first describe a situation without writing down your thoughts or feelings. Just stick to the basic facts.

Then, write your true emotional reaction and your thoughts about the situation. With your thoughts down on paper, you can then read through them to identify what cognitive distortion, or negative thought trap, you have fallen into. We cover these traps in detail in Chapter IV. Basically, all negative thoughts fall into one of these traps. Free yourself from the trap next by identifying an alternative thought pattern that is more positive. In the final part of your entry, brainstorm solutions to the situation.

You can also use this analysis for thoughts that cause you distress rather than actual life situations. These thoughts may not be in reaction to a specific situation that happened during the course of your day. Rather, they could be thoughts that constantly bother you, or that seemed to come at you out of nowhere. No thoughts actually come out of nowhere, but if it seems this way, then you need to analyze the thoughts to find their source.

These thoughts could be anything, though usually the most bothersome thoughts are about yourself or about your life in general. They could be worries and concerns. When writing about these thoughts, treat each thought as an event. Write down the thought. Then, begin the process of evaluating what mental trap this thought draws you into. Find a better alternative. Write down new thoughts that you can think whenever this hurtful thought bothers you again. Finally, you should try to see why this thought occurred to you. Was there a situation that happened right before the thought popped into your head? Did you see some sort of stimuli that sparked an association?

You may be asking yourself, "How can I get better by just writing down my thoughts and feelings? This seems awfully simple." Well, remember the mistake Dr. Allen made by dismissing the power of CBT. This simple process of writing down situations and thoughts is very useful because it provides you with an understanding of your thought processes. Analyzing all of your bad thoughts gives you a thorough understanding of your life and your mental processes. When you become aware of issues, you are in a position to find solutions to them.

Your CBT practice also does something else important: it creates a good habit. When you write down more positive alternatives to your thoughts, you begin to think about them. The more you think positively and helpfully, the more your mind learns to follow that path of thinking in the future. You can transform your mind by this simple process.

Finally, writing down your thoughts enables you to think of reasonable solutions. CBT is geared toward solving problems rather than suffering from them. Often, reasonable solutions exist, but you fail to think of them because you are more focused on how much situations hurt. By taking this new approach to situations, you are able to make your thoughts and feelings seem like simple facts. With the chatter in your brain quieted, you are free to focus your energy on how to go about solving your problems in a realistic and helpful way.

Think of CBT as becoming more helpful to yourself. You are becoming a solution-oriented person who focuses on helping yourself through bad situations. Think more helpful thoughts and do more helpful things.

Chapter IV: Cognitive Distortions

Almost all negative thoughts belong to a certain thought habit, known formally as a cognitive distortion. These different habits are not conducive to solutions. Instead, they just cause you to feel bad and send you in a downward spiral into worse thoughts. These cognitive distortions lie at the root of your unhappiness.

Many people are stuck in mental ruts. It is possible that you have developed ugly thought habits over the years. These habits route your thoughts along certain bad patterns, and cause you to think negatively all the time in reaction to all situations, lowering your mood every day. You are not inherently a negative person, but life and negative role models have made you so. Negative thought habits are often such a part of your life that they lie at the bottom of all of your thinking and manifest in your reactions to all situations in all areas of your life.

Having a negative thought habit is very bad. These thought habits cause more strife than you realize. They are also insidious because they go on in your head without your awareness. You follow the path of bad thoughts without meaning to, and you can't seem to think more positively.

Fortunately, that is how CBT can help you. Once you learn about these different bad thought habits, you can begin to identify where your unhappiness comes from. You can begin to uproot these habits and replace them with healthier thoughts habits, which are covered in

Chapter V. For every bad thought, there is an alternative thought that makes you feel better and leads you to thinking up solutions to your problems. You can develop positive thought habits instead of negative ones with some practice.

Before you begin thinking positive thoughts, find out the thoughts you have that are negative. In the following pages, we will cover major cognitive distortions and the types of thoughts that fall into these patterns. More than likely, you will find thoughts you are constantly thinking somewhere in the following pages. This can be disheartening when you realize how negative your thinking really is, but it can also be uplifting because you will realize that you are not alone, you are not broken, and you have the ability to fix your thinking using this book. An end to your misery is in sight!

If you don't find your specific thoughts in the following pages, you need to find out the cause of your bad thoughts. You don't necessarily need to know what category your negative thinking falls into to isolate a solution. If a thought seems negative or lowers your mood, then you need to change it. Find the cause of the thought and then try to find a positive thought to replace it.

Assuming

Perhaps you had an old teacher or a parent who loved to say, "When you assume, you make an ass of you and me." It probably irritated you to no end when you heard this, but there is wisdom to this annoying saying. You really can make an ass of yourself because when you assume, there is a strong possibility that you may be wrong.

Assuming means that you think something is true without any proof or confirmation of its validity. Assumptions are never proven, yet many of us treat them as solid truth. We trust our assumptions enough to act on them. But we are acting on a belief that has no authentic basis, and as a result, we can make some major mistakes with our reactions. Some other terms that mean the same thing as assuming are jumping to conclusions, miscommunicating, and misunderstanding.

When you think that something is true, you need to do some fact-checking before you act. Never assume that something is true without getting proof, no matter how convinced you feel. Don't assume that someone thinks or feels something. If you get upset about something someone says, don't assume that they meant it the way you took it in.

Here are some typical assumptions:

Your significant other says, "We need to talk." You automatically assume that he or she is about to break up with you. You start panicking and crying and trying to find out what you did wrong. Then you show up at his or her place to talk and find out it is about a career change, or something else unrelated to breaking up. You put yourself through all that worry for nothing, all over a silly assumption!

Someone in your office does not say hi to you or look at you. You assume that this person hates you. You spend your time trying to figure out why you earned his or her dislike and you feel down about the relationship. Maybe you even start treating this person in an ugly way, or you stage a confrontation. The reality is, the person doesn't say hi because he or she is extremely shy and suffers from severe social anxiety.

Your friend hosts a party and doesn't invite you. You automatically assume that you were left out because your friendship is over or because everyone hates you and you have no social skills. You get yourself down, thinking horrible thoughts about yourself and your friend. Really, you were not invited because the party was for someone you don't know, or your friend thought you were busy that night because of a previous conversation where you talked about a prior commitment. Or maybe the party was simply not your style and involved things or people that you hate. Whatever the reason, your assumption that everyone hates you was way off.

When you analyze your thoughts in your diary, realize when you are accepting something horrible as true without any hard evidence to back it up. Consider that there are alternatives to your assumption. Find out what is really going on before letting your assumption drag you down.

All-or-nothing Thinking

This thought habit is commonly associated with depression and bipolar disorder. It occurs when you think that everything is black or white. You think that everything is just wonderful, or positively horrible. You think that either everyone hates you or everyone loves you. It is normal to fall into the trap of all-or-nothing thinking because humans are naturally programmed to have the "fight or flight" instinct which requires quick decisions about a situation. But it is important to dismiss this thinking because usually it is false. You need to consider the fact that there are usually in-between gray areas in life. And usually people never feel an extreme about someone, but rather they feel ambivalence.

An example of all-or-nothing thinking is thinking that everyone hates you when you overhear a co-worker say something negative about you and another co-worker agreed. People like to talk negatively about others, and often gossip. Just because someone has a bad thing to say does not mean that everyone feels an extreme hatred toward you.

Another example is when you think about a life situation and think that it is entirely awful. You do not consider the positives to a situation or the things you have to be grateful for. You just think, "I hate this! It is awful! Why is life always horrible like this?"

Thoughts that fit into all-or-nothing thinking usually contain terms like, "always," "forever," "everyone," "everything," "total," and "completely." This is not a complete list, but you should get the gist. Any kind of thinking that puts life into terms of black and white fall into this thinking pattern.

Dwelling on Pain

Dwelling and ruminating are obviously never good. If you are focused on something that hurts you, you subject yourself to your pain constantly and you feel the pain over and over again. Remember the fact that you think seventy thousand thoughts a day? And each of those thoughts causes a subsequent emotion? Well, if you devote many of those thoughts to memories of your pain, then you are subjecting yourself to bursts of that pain throughout the day. This can really get you down and make you depressed.

Many people have the erroneous belief that thinking about their problems over and over can actually provide them with relief. This is why people with anxiety often turn to worrying as a habit. But how can you find relief if you are just focusing on your pain? You are doing nothing to find solutions. Thinking about your pain will not produce a magical solution, but instead will hold you in a place of negativity.

When you dwell on pain, you think about something that hurt you over and over. You think about things like how you could have acted differently, or how infuriated you are that someone actually had the nerve to say something to you. You feel in awe about how awful you can actually feel and you ache for a time before you experienced this pain. Maybe you feel sorry for yourself and think constantly about how pain infiltrates your life and what you have lost because of your pain. In many cases, you even use your pain as an excuse to not participate in life or to engage in behaviors that make you feel better for the short term, such as smoking.

Overgeneralizing

This cognitive distortion is characterized by the habit of drawing conclusions about things based on one small piece of evidence. You do not have enough information to draw a conclusion about something, yet you do anyway, and you accept your conclusion as total truth. These conclusions can lead you to act erroneously or avoid a great situation because you assume that it will be bad. You may adhere to certain prejudices or refer to your past experiences to draw conclusions about things that you really know nothing about. A previous bad experience may sour your mental picture of certain situations, but just because something bad happened in the past does not mean that it will bad in the future.

Really, overgeneralizing is related to assuming and also all-or-nothing thinking. You should never make assumptions about things, and you should never see only one outcome. Do not draw conclusions without sufficient evidence. You cannot predict the future. When you analyze your thoughts, look for when you are predicting the future and ask if you really have enough information to make that prediction. Different outcomes are possible in life. Not every situation is the same.

Commonly, overgeneralizing sounds like, "All men are the same. My ex often stood me up, so I know that this guy will too." You may also think things like, "All conventions like this suck. I know I will have a terrible time," or "People are generally horrible inside and have no altruistic motives for anything. This guy is going to let me down, I just know it." You may drag in prejudices, such as, "He's of this race, so he is going to act like this, it's inevitable." You may avoid a business opportunity because something similar failed for you in the past and you predict that this one has no chance of succeeding. You may avoid dating or bring in lots of baggage into relationships because you overgeneralize that all people are out to hurt you and relationships will never work out. You draw predictions about the future without giving anything a chance.

Mind Reading

Mind reading is a lot like assuming. You assume what others are thinking and feeling. You do not take the time to hear it from someone. Thinking you know just what others are thinking and why they do the things that they do can hurt you because you may be wrong. You don't know what others are thinking so don't imagine their thoughts.

The term "must" or "clearly" often come up when you perform mind reading. You think things like, "He must think I'm fat. That's why he didn't compliment me on my new dress," or "She must be thinking I was a jerk!" You think that someone treated you rudely because they think they are better than you. You may also think that someone will react to something a certain way, and you predict this reaction with certainty as if you are psychic. "She is going to be furious when she finds out!"

Analyze your thoughts for attempts at mind reading. If you find yourself rationalizing why someone did something and writing down their thoughts that they never told you they were thinking, you are performing mind reading.

Negative Self-labeling

Negative self-labeling is rather intuitive. It involves slapping labels on yourself that are negative. You believe the worst about yourself, usually because of a single failure or bad situation in the past. Your self-esteem is low because you have so much self-hatred inside and you believe that you are flawed in some way.

By thinking these negative thoughts, you hurt your chances of feeling well about yourself and loving yourself. You may ignore great opportunities because you think that you are not good enough, or you may not engage in social activities and dating because you think that you are too flawed to be lovable. You bring your doubt into relationships, work, and all other areas of life, approaching everything with a self-fulfilling prophecy that you will fail. When you talk about yourself to others, you say self-defacing things that people in turn believe. This can make others dislike you as much as you dislike yourself. By thinking negatively about yourself, you limit yourself and prevent your own happiness and success.

You think harsh things about yourself if you have this cognitive distortion. You think things like, "I am a failure," or "I am always bad at this," or "I have no social skills and I'm not interesting." When someone breaks up with you, you blame yourself because of your long laundry list of faults. When you don't get a promotion or lose a job, you think that is entirely because you are a failure.

Look for unkind thoughts about yourself in your thinking. Even the smallest self-label can hurt you tremendously. You need to treat yourself kindly and say things about yourself that you would want others to say to you. Do not say things to yourself that you would be hurt about if someone else said them to you.

Disqualifying the Positive

This is the ultimate Debbie Downer. When you disqualify the positive, you deliberately ignore or discount positive aspects of life in favor of the negative. You shun what is good in life to dwell on what is bad. This leads to missing out on the good things in life and neglecting to tend to your loved ones. You redirect every potential positive thought into a negative one.

If you think of good things and then automatically think of a way to discount them, you are engaging in this cognitive distortion. You may think things like, "This house is nice, but I hate the light in the living room" or "This is a nice view but it's a long walk. I hate walking." You may also think things like, "Life is just a big series of disappointments. This seems like a good thing, but I bet it will disappoint me, like everything else."

You need to cease disqualifying the positives. The positives are all you have to make you happy. There are many more positives than you may realize, and if you start to pay attention to them, you may be shocked by how much happier you feel.

Disqualifying the Present

When you disqualify the present, you ignore the importance of the present moment. The only moment you have to live is now. The past is over and the future is uncertain, so you need to focus on the present. Not doing so makes you miss out on your life. You neglect your present needs and what you must do in the moment for favor of a future event. Disqualifying the present can lead to anxiety and procrastination.

You can spot this cognitive distortion when you think thoughts that contain terms like, "I am so tired, but I can rest later because first I must finish this project." The word "later" is a big indicator that you are disqualifying the present. Rushing to do something for a future goal and neglecting what you really need to be doing in the present is harmful to you and shows up in the way you think about time. Focusing on the future or past and rushing through what you are currently doing indicate that you have an unhealthy relationship with time.

It is time to slow down and appreciate life. The present is the only real time that you have, so make the best of it. Stop focusing on the future so much.

"Should" Thinking

"She should have done this" or "I should have said this" are examples of should thinking. Should thinking is when you believe that the world and other people should operate a specific way. You also develop unrealistic expectations for the future and set yourself up for great pain when something does not meet them. When things do not go the way you believe they should, you drown in regret and dwell on the past.

"Should" thinking can underlie a lot of anger issues.

If you hold this kind of thinking, you set yourself up for constant rude awakenings when the world does not go your way. You will devote a massive amount of time to thinking of how things should have gone or should go, rather than focusing on finding solutions to the damage from situations that went poorly.

In your diary, spot "should" phrases. Those are the phrases you need to change! Erase "should" from your mental vocabulary.

Pessimism

Pessimism is a dark mental hole of misery. No one loves a pessimist. Pessimists always bring the mood down. If you engage in pessimistic thinking, you are only bringing your own mood down, as well as everyone else's. When you engage in pessimistic thinking, you automatically disqualify all positives and resign yourself to the viewpoint that life is horrible and miserable.

You think things like, "Life is horrible, and none of us are meant to be happy. We are all just born to die." You automatically approach everything from an angle of doom and sorrow. Just reading your thoughts in your diary or on your workbook should make it clear if you are pessimistic. Try being optimistic for once and you will start to see that life is not so bad.

Blaming Others

Failing to take responsibility for yourself and blaming your problems on others cripples your ability to make solutions for your problems. You think that others are responsible for everything wrong in your life, and so others must fix everything. But no one can fix anything for you. Even if someone does wrong you, it is unfortunately up to you to fix the situation to the best of your ability.

You cannot blame others for what is wrong in your life. Only you have the power to make your life great. You must take responsibility for it in order to change it. Relying on others will only disappoint you and you will live in a constant state of anxiety, anger, and depression.

Look for thoughts where you say to yourself, "If only so-and-so had done this" or "Thanks to so-and-so, I'm now screwed." When other people come into your thoughts as the causes of your issues, you need to eliminate those thoughts. Instead think of what you did in the situation and how you can handle it better in the future. Focus on finding solutions to difficult relationships, rather than casting blame.

Excessive Need for Approval

It is natural to want to please your loved ones. Approval feels good and validates your efforts. But constantly desiring and seeking the approval of others can drive you crazy and make you very anxious and depressed. Not everyone is going to approve of you. You will find yourself constantly doubting yourself as you jump through hoops for other people.

Examples of this cognitive distortion are when you blame yourself for upsetting someone or blame yourself for someone else's bad mood. If you think things like, "I need to buy this so I look good to other men," you are thinking only of how to gain approval from others.

Instead of seeking others' approval, seek to approve of yourself. Do things for you. Work on your goals, rather than others' goals. Make sure that your thoughts about yourself remain positive.

Catastrophizing

Catastrophizing is the annoying thing that drama queens do. "My hair isn't perfect. It's the end of the world!" But you may engage in this silly dramatizing yourself without even realizing it. You focus all of your energy on blowing a situation up into something terrible, rather than thinking of reasonable solutions. You treat situations as if they are unsolvable, and will result in your ultimate ruin.

If you feel like difficulties in life signify the end of the world and are a cause for feelings of doom and despair, you are catastrophizing. Look at the hard situations in your life and consider how you think about them. Do you think things like, "This is horrible! I will never be able to pay rent on time because my car just broke down"? You are catastrophizing your car breaking down. It can be a major hiccup in your financial health, but it is usually not the end. You should dedicate your energy to finding a solution rather than thinking that everything is the end of the world. You are tougher than you think and you will probably survive this situation.

Chapter V: Realistic and Healthy Thinking

The negative thought patterns that we covered in the previous chapter are not helpful or realistic. Instead of helping you feel better and find solutions to your problems, they instead drag you into a whirlpool of negativity and misery. Realistic, positive, and solution-oriented thoughts are more helpful in handling life. They will uplift you and allow you to find ideal solutions.

When you find out what your negative thoughts are in your journal or in your workbook, you can start to change them. Convert all negative thoughts to more positive ones. When I say positive, I am not just referring to happy thinking. I am referring to helpful thinking. Think thoughts that help you find solutions, rather than thoughts that hurt you. Solutions will help you feel better as you begin to improve your life's situations.

Here are some examples of positive alternatives to negative thoughts.

Assuming

Convert assumptions to thinking, "I don't know this for sure. Maybe I should verify this belief I have before I act on it?" It is best to take a deep breath when you start to get worked up over assumptions. Do not obsess and feel hurt over things that you simply assume.

Assumptions are easy to believe because they have some level of likelihood. It is possible that your assumptions are correct. But you should not base too much emotion or energy on your assumptions. If your assumptions do prove to be true, focus on how to handle the situation.

All-or-nothing thinking

Start to see life in shades of gray. Things are so rarely black and white. Things may not be as extreme as you think. Removing the extremity from situations can result in less anxiety and a clearer mind. You stop overreacting and you start to calm down with the understanding that life is not so bad. You also stop thinking that everything will be perfect, a belief which is bound to let you down.

Research has shown that depressed people generally get happier more easily. It does not take much to make a depressed person bounce up from a low mood. Therefore, depressed people can experience a great deal of ups and downs. They feel amazing and crash down to feeling horrible. Balanced emotions are far healthier. Try to approach things with a balance perspective. Accept that there will be bad along with the good and vice versa.

Also try adding some calmness to your life. Relaxation exercises can be a good step. Relax and scale back on the emotional extremism that you are used to.

Dwelling on Pain

Think of the good things in life. Think of what makes you feel good. You can also engage in some type of pleasure-giving opportunity. But you do not need to drown in your pain because there are many better emotions that you can feel. Dwelling is not the way to feel better. Consider bereavement counseling.

Overgeneralizing

Consider that this time things might be different. Not everything in life is the same. You may have just found the pot of gold at the end of the rainbow. You can guard your heart, but you don't have to imprison it. Approach scary situations with caution, but don't avoid them altogether out of fear that they will turn out exactly like a previous situation.

Negative Self-Labeling

For every flaw inside of you, there are a million good things. You may also be exaggerating the bad things that you think about yourself. Start thinking along the lines of, "I am a good person. I am beautiful, and strong." Think of good things that you do or have done for the world and things that you are good at.

Also, take this as a time to reflect on what you want to change about yourself. We all have flaws and fixing our flaws are important to our growth. Maybe your negative self-labeling is a sign that you have some things to change.

Disqualifying the Positive

Start accepting that the positive is real. You may be afraid of embracing the positive because from experience you know that all good things must end. But why should you subject yourself to constant misery? Enjoy the good things while they last. Start to enjoy the positive and always think of the positives in any situation, no matter how hard it may be.

Disqualifying the Present

Think of how you can enjoy the present. What do you need right now? What should you handle now rather than later? Stop putting things off and take proactive action in the present. This is the surest way to avoid regrets in the future. The only day you have to live right now is today.

"Should" Thinking

You are not the queen or king of the universe. Your idea of how things should go is not law and you will often be let down by your expectations. Begin to relax your rules and think,

"Well, it didn't go how it should have, but I can't help that. Now I need to move on and find solutions."

When considering worries about the future, stop thinking "Things should go this way" and instead think "I don't know how this will go but here is what I hope for." Hope is uplifting and much better than the rigidity of should thinking.

Pessimism

Try optimism for once! Think that sometimes life is great and some people really are happy. If others can be happy, why can't you? Begin to think more positively and have hope instead of constant despair.

Blaming Others

You can think all day about how people could have behaved differently, but you cannot change their actions. Instead, think of how you could have handled the situation differently. Most likely, there is a way that you can handle things without drama and conflict. Finding what you did wrong in a situation can help you find ways to fix it.

This is not to say that everything is your fault! There are jerks out there and sometimes others make mistakes that hurt you badly. But you can do damage control when others hurt you. Instead of blaming them, simply forgive them. Put distance between yourself and people that cause you troubles. Work on your conflict resolution and communication skills. Brainstorm ways that you can overcome differences and heal from hurt caused by other people.

Mind Reading

You cannot read others' minds. When you find yourself mind reading, remind yourself that you are not a mind reader and that you may be wrong. Consider asking someone what they are thinking. If you can't do that for whatever reason, consider the fact that you can stop thinking about what another person is thinking. Do they really have that much importance in your life? Do their thoughts really count that much and deserve that much of your energy and time?

Excessive Need for Approval

You need to approve of yourself. Rarely do other people's opinions matter that much. Do their opinions pay your bills or make you happy? Would their disapproval truly kill you? Do they have that much importance in your life? And do you have much importance in theirs? Probably not. Therefore, you need to stop focusing on their approval.

Some people's opinions do matter. You need to please your boss or your clients. You need to maintain affection with your partner. But rarely do you need to worry about whether or not other people like you. You can separate your need for approval in the workplace from your need for approval personally. Keep seeking approval in areas where it is important, but eliminate needing approval to bolster your ego in areas that do not matter so badly.

Catastrophizing

There are true catastrophes that create a high level of emotional distress. If you lose a home to a fire or a loved one to an accident, you have a right to feel overwhelmed and horrified. But feeling this way over daily trials and inconveniences is totally unnecessary. When you start to catastrophize, consider how dire this situation really is. Are you in danger? Will you truly lose everything? Will this be the end of your life? Most likely, it is not so bad.

Think of how you can resolve issues instead of thinking about how horrible they are. There is almost always a solution to every sticky situation. But often you need to dedicate some energy to finding a solution and so you need to reserve your energy from emotional spiraling and refocus it on finding how to work out an issue.

Chapter VI: Finding Situations to Avoid

It may seem like common sense, to avoid situations that make you hurt inside. But unfortunately, many people do not always realize what specific situations cause them sadness, anger, and anxiety. A very useful part of CBT is identifying the specific situations that do cause your negative thoughts and emotions to manifest. Once you know what to avoid, you can begin to eliminate the sources of misery in your life.

There are often toxic people in life that get you into ugly situations and mess with your happiness. Sometimes these people are close friends, lovers, or family members. You need to look at what people bring into your life. Are there certain people that just seem to always lower your mood? Do you spend an afternoon with a friend, and suddenly find yourself full of anxiety and doubt? Does your partner make you feel inadequate, like you must scramble and jump through hoops to earn his or her approval? Do you have a friend or relative who constantly needs help and is always asking you for money, a place to stay, or something else that requires your energy?

You do not need people in your life that hurt you. People who suck your energy, make you doubt yourself, cause you drama, or otherwise mess up your sunny days do not belong in your life. It is time for them to go. You need to take care of yourself and surrounding yourself with negative people is not good for self-care.

If there are people in your life that consistently seem to bring you down or lead you into poor situations, it is time to put distance. It can hurt tremendously to part ways with certain people, but having them in your life is actually hurting you much more.

You should also analyze your life for situations that bring out your symptoms. These situations are commonly known as triggers. Triggers may be very obvious because they cause an immediate emotional response. If you notice an association between a type of situation and a mood change, you need to try to avoid that type of situation in the future.

But some triggers are more subtle. You will find yourself suddenly depressed, anxious, unable to control your anger, or craving a substance and you have no idea why. These symptoms do not just manifest out of nothing. They have a source.

Think back on what happened throughout the day, especially around the time your symptoms manifested. You can use your journal for this. Did you ever feel a bite of angst when something happened, no matter how small? Did you hear a song that reminded you of a bad time in your life or someone important that you lost? Did you see someone today that you normally don't see? Think over situations and how they made you feel. If something stands out to you, it could be the source of your symptoms, even if it doesn't make sense as the cause.

When you isolate situations that give rise to your mental illness symptoms, you need to work hard to avoid those situations in the future. If large crowds throw you into an anxiety tailspin, try to avoid crowds and leave for work before or after rush hour. If certain people bring you down, do not see them if you can help it. If certain music or movies remind you of painful memories, don't turn to them for entertainment and turn the radio down when a certain song comes on.

Unfortunately, not all situations are avoidable. Some situations that cause your symptoms may be part of your everyday life or may be necessary on certain occasions. Toxic people may be an everyday staple in your life and you cannot reasonably just run away. It is OK to avoid situations and people that bring you harm for a happier life, but running away from your problems is not what CBT preaches. We will talk more about how to handle facing unavoidable situations and people in the next chapter. There is a way to cope with the unavoidable and necessary trials of life.

In addition, diet, drinking water, and exercise can have big impacts on your mental wellness. Links have been discovered between behavior and certain foods, including dyes, preservatives, artificial sweeteners, gluten, and dairy. While these behavioral changes are usually observed most keenly in children, they can affect adults too. How well did you eat today? Is there a particular food that seems to bring out your worst moods?

Also, did you drink at least eight glasses of water? Dehydration can be a factor in depression and irritability.

Sleep is also important for mood health. A good eight hours of uninterrupted slumber is best for your ideal functioning the next day. Sleep allows your body to repair itself and allows your brain to reset mentally. Dreams can help you process events from the previous day and have a surprisingly profound effect on your brain's ability to recover from emotional damage. There is a reason that people say, "Sleep on it." If you didn't sleep enough, your symptoms may be harder to manage the following day. Your yucky mood may be because you are physically exhausted and your brain has not had time to unwind and heal from the trials and tribulations of yesterday.

It may seem silly to talk about diet and sleep in a book about CBT. But CBT is all about caring for yourself. Taking care of your physical health has a profound effect on your mental health. After all, there is a strong link between the body and the mind. CBT encourages its users to tend to their physical needs and work on staying fit and healthy.

Chapter VII: Coping with the Unavoidable

Avoiding situations that bring you harm is great. But in real life, we both know that that is not always realistic. Life throws plenty of bad situations at you and you can't avoid them all. Therefore, it is essential to develop healthy coping skills for when you do encounter these situations.

Situations that stir up mental illness symptoms can be everyday situations that other, healthier people find to be no big deal. But for you, they can feel catastrophic. They can lead you to relapse in your symptoms, after working so hard to overcome those symptoms with CBT. Learning to cope in harmful everyday situations is essential to keep yourself from falling into despair.

Anxiety

Many everyday situations that are nothing to healthy people can trigger severe anxiety in some. For instance, a huge crowd at an airport can be stressful for anyone, but it can be disastrous for you if you have agoraphobia or social anxiety. But what if you have to fly for work or to visit a sick relative? You have to be a part of that airport crowd, whether you like it or not. The situation is not ideal for you but you can use various techniques to cope with your anxiety.

The best technique is relaxation. Focus on your breathing. Breathe in through your nose, out through your mouth. By focusing on your breathing, you take your mind off of the stress that surrounds it.

Progressive muscle relaxation also is helpful in anxiety-provoking situations. First start with the muscles in your scalp. Force yourself to relax those muscles. Next move to your forehead muscles. Keep roving your mind over your body, forcing the relaxation of each of your muscle groups. The relaxation will calm you and the intense mental focus required to perform this exercise will take your mind off of your stress.

Some people find tapping to be soothing. You can repeat a mantra to yourself such as, "I will survive this. This is really not so bad" as you tap different parts of your body. The physical action of tapping paired with the repeated affirmation can help trick your mind into believing what you are saying to yourself.

Sometimes anxiety can impair your ability to focus on anything. In that case, it is essential to pick a spot on the wall and focus on it intently. Do not chase any other thoughts that enter your head. That spot on the wall is your refuge. Use it to take your mind off of the craziness raging around you and within you.

Facing Your Fears

CBT is great for helping you overcome irrational fears and phobias. This is because CBT allows you to think about your phobias and understand that they are not rational and not conducive to your peace of mind.

If you have a phobia, you may find it very helpful to write about your phobia. When it is on paper, you will begin to see how silly it really is. If you are scared of airplanes, what are the odds of a crash, really? You are far more likely to die in a car crash than a plane crash. If you are scared of dogs because of a traumatic encounter with a dog in your childhood, remember that most dogs are man's best friends and that you are a lot bigger now. Analyze your fears to see how scary they really are.

To truly overcome your phobia, you need to begin to condition yourself to it. Exposing yourself to what scares you can help teach your mind to stop fearing it as it witnesses you emerge unscathed. There are classes you can take to condition yourself to overcome fear of heights, flying, and other phobias. Consider going to the snake or spider exhibit at a local zoo to stand near the creatures that make you want to scream. You will begin to realize that your phobias do not hurt you. If you have social phobia, try taking brief walks outside and striking up a brief conversation with one stranger a day.

The above relaxation techniques can also really help you when you are feeling the vise grip of fear from a phobia. Breathe, focus, and use progressive muscle relaxation to bring yourself out of your fear.

Handling Depression

The hardest part of coping with depression is that depression cripples your will to do anything. You may not even have the energy to get out of bed, let alone perform CBT on yourself. But coping with your depression gets easier when you begin to change your thinking to more positive thoughts. Positive thinking has the ability to release feel-good hormones like serotonin in your brain, allowing you to feel better and begin to move forward with your life.

When you find yourself drowning in depression symptoms, there may be a reason that you feel so blue. Maybe life is just hard right now or you have not been taking care of your body. Try to identify the source of your depression and remove it from your life. Focus on the present and enjoying life right now. Life is too short to be spent suffering in your bed.

Anger Management

If you have trouble managing your anger, you need to step back and breathe when you start to see red. Use your CBT journal to write down why a situation made you mad enough to hit someone or have an outburst. Then, analyze the situation. Was it really what you thought, or were you doing something like assuming and negative labeling? Were you ignoring the positives of the situation, or of a person that angered you? Now, in the future, how can you handle this situation without hitting and throwing things and lashing out verbally? Is there something you can do that is more conducive to a reasonable solution?

Rarely is anger ever a solution. Uncontrolled anger can get you into a lot of trouble with loved ones and even the law.

Breathe, and think of better ways to react to situations than angry outbursts.

Using CBT to Overcome addiction

Addiction is often referred to as an illness. Many people fail to understand that addiction is usually a symptom of a deeper illness. People use drugs, alcohol, and other addictive behaviors such as gambling to create instant gratification and numb themselves against life. These addictive behaviors offer addicts temporary pleasure that drowns out the deeper pain addicts are experiencing inside of themselves. Basically, addicts use their addictions to distract themselves, or numb themselves, from what is really wrong. When the pleasure wears off, addicts literally feel like they are in hell because they have no shield from their pain, and they desperately chase a new high or thrill to keep them in the numb, pleased state that lets them ignore their problems. Addicts often live in denial of their real problems, and engage in harmful behaviors to avoid feeling the emotional fallout from their life situations, past traumas, or their childhoods.

Since CBT can address inner thoughts and thus change outer behaviors, it offers a rich opportunity for addicts to overcome their addictions. Addicts can use CBT to identify the thoughts and emotions that drive them to use and replace those thoughts and emotions with healthier ones that do not drive them to seek numbness. It also helps them learn to avoid situations, also known as triggers, that lead to relapses. In addition, addicts can use CBT to find healthy alternatives to self-medicating using

substances, shopping, gambling, eating, sex, or

whatever vice they have chosen to escape their

problems with.

Identify addictive behaviors and the

thoughts behind them. If you suddenly crave a

drug, what triggered you to want to use? Was it a

tense situation, like an argument with your

family or a rough day at work? Did you see

someone or hear a song from your drug days that

made your brain start thinking about drugs?

Now, think of better ways to cope with the

current situation. Maybe you can do yoga or

exercise to relieve stress. Maybe just writing in

your journal and taking a hot shower is all you

need. Engage in healthy feel-good coping

mechanisms, rather than participating in

substance use. While substance use can relieve your bad feelings in the short term, it only worsens your mental health and your life circumstances in the long term.

Above all, remember your resolve to be clean and sober. You have made tremendous progress. Your life and your health are probably significantly better without drugs and alcohol playing a role in your behavior. You don't want to backtrack now and discount everything that you have accomplished. One way to deal with cravings and addiction is to remember why you wanted to get clean in the first place. Remind yourself of the awful things about drug use that made you want to quit. Then, think about all that you have accomplished in getting clean. You have done something that less than fourteen

percent of drug users do.

Chapter VIII: Coping with Relapses

When you have a mental illness, relapse is a possibility. Relapse is often a constant source of fear for people. Unfortunately, this fear is grounded on reality. Life can throw some serious curveballs and a predisposition to negative thinking can make you succumb to mental illness again in response to emotional events.

Often people hear the term relapse and they imagine a dramatic return back to sickness. They imagine junkies blowing entire paychecks on drugs or cancer patients finding out that malignant cells are present in their bloodstream again. But a mental illness relapse is sometimes much subtler. Just a return of a persistent negative thought can count as a relapse. Maybe you start to feel bad again, or you start to worry about little things and blowing them up into big things again. Maybe you have an angry outburst. The littlest signs of your old mental habits can make you question your wellness and your ability to control your thoughts.

No matter how subtle or dramatic a relapse is, it can make you feel like you have failed. You may think that you are an incurable case and there is no hope. The emotions that accompany relapses are often overwhelming and can send you into a downward spiral that only worsens your mental condition.

But don't despair. Understand that you may relapse again and again. There are ways that you can prevent relapses. You can also bring yourself out of a relapse, should one occur.

Be Gentle on Yourself

Despite social stigmas that treat mental illness lightly, mental illness is very real. Scientific research has shown differences between the neurochemical activity of healthy "normal" human brains and human brains suffering from depression, schizophrenia, and other mental disturbances. A marked chemical difference exists between healthy and unhealthy brains. This difference shows how mental illness truly does affect the human body and thought.

If you suffer from any type of mental illness, your illness is very real. You are sick. Just like a person in the hospital for kidney failure or cancer, you suffer from malignant symptoms and you need treatment. CBT can be your best course of action, but even with CBT your risk of relapse still exists. You must keep in mind that your symptoms are not normal and that you require special self-care.

Accepting the reality of a relapse is OK. This acceptance gives you the power to take steps to avoid relapse, instead of growing complacent in being well and thinking that everything will be perfect forever. It also allows you to be gentle on yourself should a relapse occur.

Relapsing is not your fault. You have not failed. CBT is not a joke that does not work for you. Instead, you simply lost control. That is OK. You can gain control again. Instead of beating yourself up, you need to love yourself and treat yourself with the tender care that you would treat a patient in the hospital or a loved one with the flu.

Practice CBT Every Day

Like a martial art, CBT requires your strength and time to develop your thinking and coping skills. Once you develop these skills, you cannot just become complacent and think that you are safe from your mental symptoms forever. You can lose these skills over time if you do not continue practicing them. Technically, CBT is a habit, and can even be considered a lifestyle. Therefore, to remain a habit, you must keep practicing CBT even when you feel well. CBT requires constant dedication for the rest of your life.

While the term "constant dedication" may seem intimidating and overwhelming, it is not. Just keeping your CBT journal at the end or beginning of the day, and turning to your journal when times get hard, can be enough to help you keep your thoughts organized. You do not have to work tirelessly 24/7 to keep negative thoughts out of your head. You simply need to realize when you have a negative thought and replace it with a better thought. When positive thinking becomes a habit, the work you have to do to replace thoughts will become easier. But sometimes you will still need to correct certain thought patterns that lead you to a bad place.

CBT can become a very relieving part of your routine. At the end of the day or after a negative event, writing in your journal can help you relax. As you record your thoughts, identify bad thought patterns, and convert your thoughts to positive ones, the relief and peace that you feel can make all your angst melt away. It truly can be a pleasure to keep practicing CBT. You will not likely find a reason to stop practicing.

Have a Daily Routine

A daily routine is a great way to prevent relapses and guide you through a relapse should you have one. A routine is especially helpful for people with anxiety or addictions. When you have a set routine to guide you throughout the day, you can feel more certain of yourself and your life. You will get a sense of control. This can certainly help relieve the fear and instability that often leads to anxiety.

Routine can be boring. You don't have to do the same exact things every day at the same exact time. Some people find living such a measured lifestyle great, but most people find it restricting and boring. Instead of having a restrictive routine, you can create a gentle routine that helps guide you throughout your day. Try to get up at the same times, do certain workouts on specific days of the week, and eat meals around the same time. If you begin to experience anxiety, think of something that you should be doing at that time. Should you be watering your plants, walking the dog, or working out? If you have a daily task to do at that particular time in your routine, you can focus your mental energy on doing that task, rather than worrying and engaging in anxiety.

It is also good to go to bed around the same time every night and perform the same activities before you go to bed. Start a bedtime ritual. A bedtime ritual has the added benefit of helping you sleep. Find activities that soothe you and relax you before you lay down to go to sleep. You can write about your day in your CBT journal, take a bubble bath or shower, and do something like Tai Chi or yoga. Be sure to avoid caffeine six hours before bed and food at least thirty minutes before bed. Getting a good night's sleep is an important part of your routine and will make you feel better overall.

Take Time for Yourself

You need time for yourself so that you can feel validated as a person and tend to your personal needs. Many people make the mistake of neglecting themselves. Moms and busy workers are especially guilty of this. While your selflessness is wonderful, it hurts you more than you realize. You need to treat yourself with tender love and care, especially while you are suffering from mental illness or recovering from an addiction.

You do not need to take whole days off from work just to tend to your emotional needs. A simple fifteen minutes to write in your journal and a bath are sufficient. Or take some time to do a craft or a hobby that you enjoy. Whatever you do, make sure that you enjoy your time. You just need to have a moment to release the stress of your life. You live with this stress every minute of every day so a few moments without it on your shoulders will not be the end of the world.

Every day, make sure that you dedicate some time each day to you and only you. Be totally selfish for just a short while. Explain to your family, friends, or co-workers that you need just a little alone time.

Taking "you time" lets you take care of yourself. It also validates your needs as a person to yourself and to those around you. You begin to realize your personal needs and your right to take care of those needs. Having this self-love and care can help you avoid a relapse because you will feel happier and you will be taking care of yourself.

What to Do if You Relapse

If you do have a relapse, you can use CBT to bring yourself out of it. Turn to your trusty journal and write about the relapse. Identify the thoughts you have about it and work them into positive thoughts of gentleness and self-love.

Don't catastrophize a relapse and don't negatively self-label yourself. Sure, a relapse can be disheartening, but it is not the end of the world and it does not make you a failure. Be sure to think along the lines of, "I am suffering right now and I think that I have relapsed. This disappoints me, but it is not the end of the world. I overcame my problem before and now I can again."

It is also essential that you analyze your relapse to find out what led to it. Sometimes the answer is obvious, and sometimes it is not. But finding the cause of your relapse can help you avoid it in the future. Look back on your day and think of the situations that occurred and the thoughts you have been having. Likely something negative is going on that is bringing you down.

Many things can lead to a relapse. Not all of these situations are avoidable. This is why you have developed coping skills. Always use them to work through bad situations and upsetting revelations. Never be afraid to turn to your journal to help you regulate your thinking about negative events and brainstorm some coping skills that you can use to turn a bad situation around.

The most important thing about relapsing is to not give up on CBT. You need it now more than ever. Keep using your coping skills and positive thinking. They really can help you manage your symptoms and overcome your relapse.

Conclusion

Now you have reached the end of this book, but not the end of your CBT journey. These pages have prepared you to use CBT to transform your mind and consequently your life. That does not mean that your journey is over; rather, it has just begun. CBT is your best friend. It is a companion that you should carry with you through the rest of your life. Keep using it to see marked changes in how you approach life and how you feel.

Using CBT can help you in so many ways. You will likely begin to see results immediately when you begin addressing your problems in your CBT journal or workbook. Just writing down events and finding new ways of looking at them can offer you a great deal of relief and can free you from the emotional burden that negative thinking puts on you.

Remember that relapses are OK and revisit this book if you relapse to freshen your mental fortitude. Life is hard and you struggle more than most people with certain mood disorders. That does not mean that there is no hope for you. Just revisit these pages to freshen your determination to feel better and remind yourself of coping skills that you may be forgetting.

Your mind is amazing. You think over seventy thousand thoughts a day! So start making those thoughts positive and conducive to solutions today using CBT.

Sources

All or Nothing, or "Black and White" Thinking and Depression. (2016). *Clinical Depression.* Retrieved from

http://www.clinicaldepression.co.uk/dlp/understanding-depression/all-or-nothing-or-black-and white-thinking-and-depression/

CBT Self-Help Course. (2016). *Get Self Help.* Retrieved from

http://www.getselfhelp.co.uk/step1.htm

Leahy, Robert. (2011). *Cognitive-Behavioral Therapy: Proven Effectiveness.*
        Psychology Today. Retrieved from https://www.psychologytoday.com blog/anxiety-files/201111/cognitive-behavioral-therapy-proven-effectiveness.

Negative Thinking. (n.d.). *Cognitive Therapy Guide.* Retrieved from

http://www.cognitivetherapyguide.org/negative-thinking-patterns.htm.

www.ingramcontent.com/pod-product-compliance
Lightning Source LLC
Chambersburg PA
CBHW050406290526
45786CB00003B/1148

* 9 7 8 1 5 3 9 0 6 3 2 7 8 *